Building Blocks

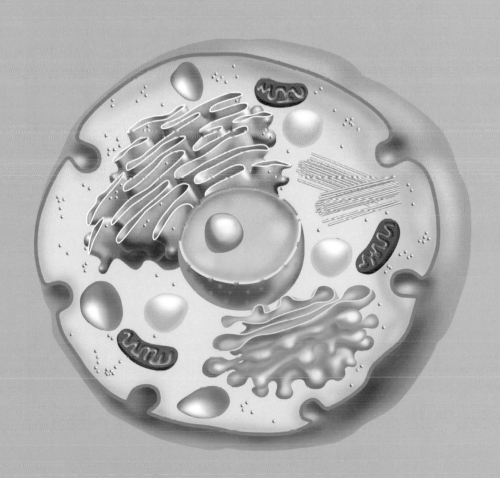

BODYSCOPE

Building Blocks

Cells, organs, and body systems

Dr. Patricia Macnair

Consultant:
Richard Walker

KINGFISHER

BOSTON

KINGFISHER

a Houghton Mifflin Company imprint
222 Berkeley Street
Boston, Massachusetts 02116
www.houghtonmifflinbooks.com

First published in 2005
10 9 8 7 6 5 4 3 2 1
1TR/0205/PROSP/PICA(PICA)/140MA/C

LIBRARY OF CONGRESS CATALOGING-IN-
PUBLICATION DATA
Macnair, Patricia Ann, 1958–
Building blocks/Patricia Macnair.—1st ed.
p. cm.—(Bodyscope)
Includes index.
1. Human physiology—
Juvenile literature.

I. Title.
QP37.M343 2005
612—dc22
2004018722

ISBN 0-7534-5792-X 1
ISBN 978-07534-5792-4

Printed in China

Author: Dr. Patricia Macnair
Consultant: Richard Walker
Editor: Clive Wilson
Designer: Peter Clayman
Illustrators: Sebastian Quigley, Guy Smith
Picture researcher: Kate Miller
Production controller: Lindsey Scott
DTP coordinator: Sarah Pfitzner
DTP operator: Primrose Burton
Indexer: Sue Lightfoot

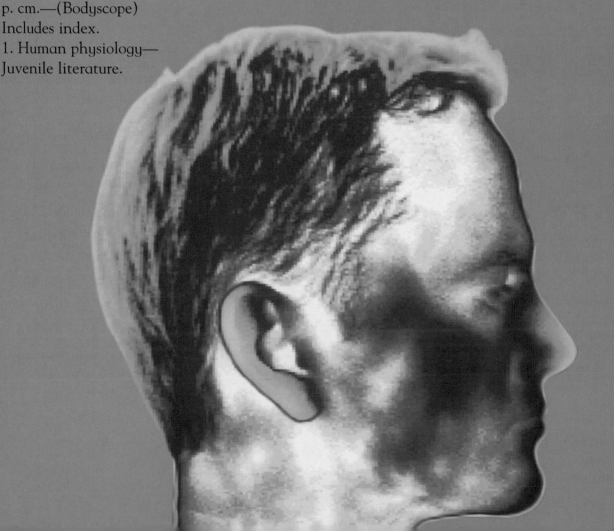

Contents

Our bodies

Every person in the world is unique. Humans come in many shapes and sizes. We have different skin, hair, and eye colors. But under the skin our working parts are very similar to everyone else's.

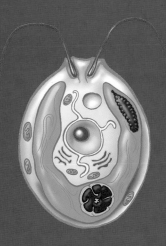

▲ Humans are made up of millions of cells, but some microscopic living things, such as this one, only have a single cell.

The smallest unit

All living things are made up of cells. Cells are so tiny that they can only be seen with a microscope. Some organisms, such as bacteria, are made of up just one cell. It takes millions and millions of cells to build an organism like the human body.

▼ Only humans have the skills and intelligence needed to create buildings like this art gallery in Bilbao, Spain.

Busy body

The human body is as complex as a large town. Food and oxygen supplies must be taken in and carried to every body part, and waste has to be taken away. Messages are sent around the body and to the outside world, and defense against invaders is vital.

Even though humans are all made in the same general pattern, no one looks exactly the same as any other person.

Let's create

Although we are made of cells like every other living thing, we have features that set us apart. Our brains are highly developed, and because we stand on two legs, we can use our hands to carry out complicated tasks. This has allowed us to shape our surroundings, to build civilizations, and to explore space.

Groups

In the body cells of the same type group together to form tissue such as fat or muscle. Organs, such as the heart, are formed when tissues join together. A group of organs working together on one job, such as breathing or digestion, is called a system.

Info lab

- The first living organism appeared on Earth around 3.8 billion years ago.

- The human body contains around 100 trillion cells.

- There are more than six billion people on our planet.

Cells

A cell is the smallest unit of life. Tiny parts inside each cell work together like machinery to make it come alive. A nucleus, or control center, tells this machinery what to do. Tiny power plants, called mitochondria, release energy to keep the cell running.

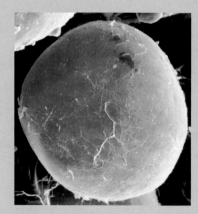

▲ A nerve cell has many branches that make contact with other nerve cells.

Cell shapes

Cells come in many shapes and sizes depending on the job they are designed to do. Nerve cells, which stretch through the body and carry important signals, are usually long and thin. Fat cells are often round and packed full of stored energy from food.

cytoplasm, a watery jelly that supports organelles

Recipe for life

Every cell nucleus contains tiny "packages" of information called chromosomes. These are made of a substance called DNA. DNA is like a cookbook that has all the instructions needed to make a complete human body.

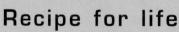

▲ This is a fat cell magnified 700 times. A layer of fat cells under the skin helps insulate the body, keeping you warm.

◀ If you could unravel a chromosome, it would look like a spiraling ladder.

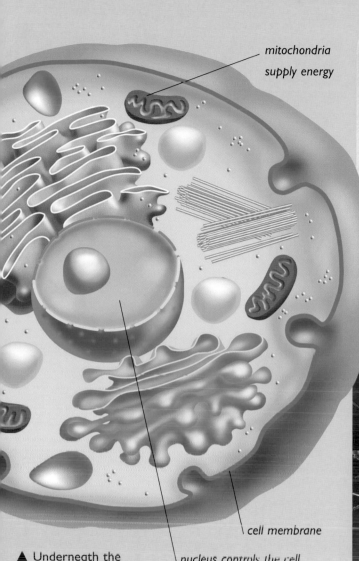

mitochondria
supply energy

cell membrane

nucleus controls the cell

▲ Underneath the membrane, or surface, of a cell, tiny structures—called organelles—are hard at work.

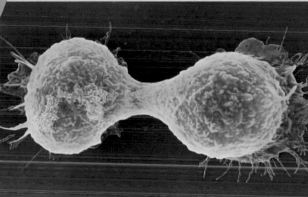

▲ This picture, magnified hundreds of times, shows a cell dividing in half. In this way the body can replace cells that become damaged or die.

Red and white

Most cells stay firmly in one place. But some cells can roam around the body. Red blood cells in the blood carry oxygen to cells around the body and remove waste from them. White blood cells can move through the tissues to attack invaders such as bacteria.

Cycle of cells

Every second millions of cells in your body are dying or becoming damaged. Some cells, such as those in your skin or lining your intestines, are lost very quickly. Fortunately, almost all of the cells in the body are able to reproduce, or divide to form new cells.

From cell to system

Cells are the body's building blocks. The billions and billions of cells that make up your body are carefully organized. Cells of a similar type group together to form tissues. And different types of tissues work together to form organs.

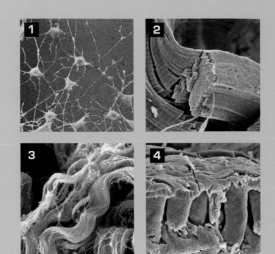

▲ The body has four main types of tissues: nervous tissue (1), muscle tissue (2), connective tissue (3), and epithelial tissue (4).

◄ Cells are the smallest units that make up the human body.

◄ Tissues are made from a group of cells of the same type that are packed together.

◄ An organ, like the liver, is formed from two or more types of tissues.

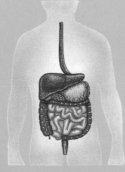

◄ The body has several systems. Each system contains two or more organs that work as a team.

Different jobs

Each type of tissue performs its own jobs. Connective tissue supports and joins parts of the body. Another type, called epithelium, lines the inside and outside of the body. It stops invaders from getting in and liquids from flowing out.

Listen up!

Most organs are tucked inside your body where you cannot see them. But you may be able to feel or even hear them at work. Listen to your stomach rumble when you are hungry or feel your heart thump after you have been running.

Teamwork

When two or more organs work together to get a specific job done, they are called a system. For example, the respiratory system is made up of all of the organs that help bring oxygen into the body. This includes the nose, breathing tubes, and the lungs.

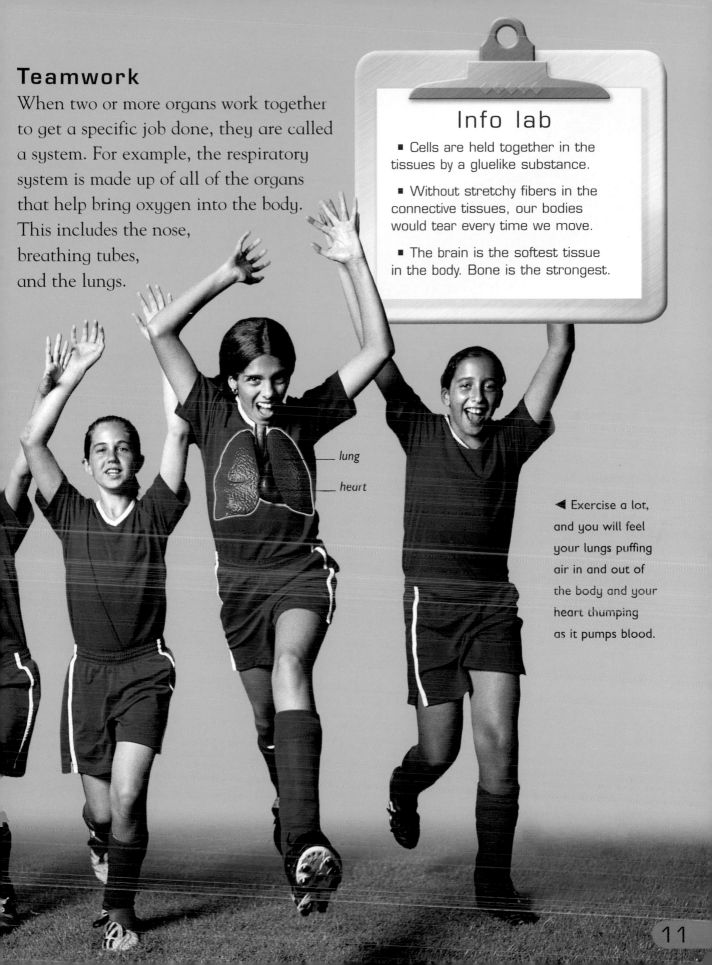

Info lab

- Cells are held together in the tissues by a gluelike substance.

- Without stretchy fibers in the connective tissues, our bodies would tear every time we move.

- The brain is the softest tissue in the body. Bone is the strongest.

lung

heart

◄ Exercise a lot, and you will feel your lungs puffing air in and out of the body and your heart thumping as it pumps blood.

Creatures at home on your body

▲ These orange threads are a fungus that causes athlete's foot. This makes the skin between the toes very itchy.

Get ready to squirm! You share your body with millions of other living things. Your insides are teeming with bacteria, and your hair and skin are home to tiny mites and other organisms. But most, you'll be pleased to know, are harmless.

▼ Billions of bacteria of all shapes and sizes cover the skin. They help keep out more harmful microorganisms.

Invasion of the fungi

Most people have tiny fungi growing on their skin, feeding on the oils that the skin produces. But if the surface of the skin is broken by a cut or scrape, these organisms can become harmful and cause problems such as athlete's foot.

▲ You share your body with a variety of creatures, including bacteria in your intestines (1), skin fungi (2), eyelash mites (3), and sometimes head lice (4).

Wash your hands

Some bacteria that live in the intestines are good for you and release vitamins. But if you don't wash your hands after going to the bathroom, bacteria can end up on the food you touch and make you sick.

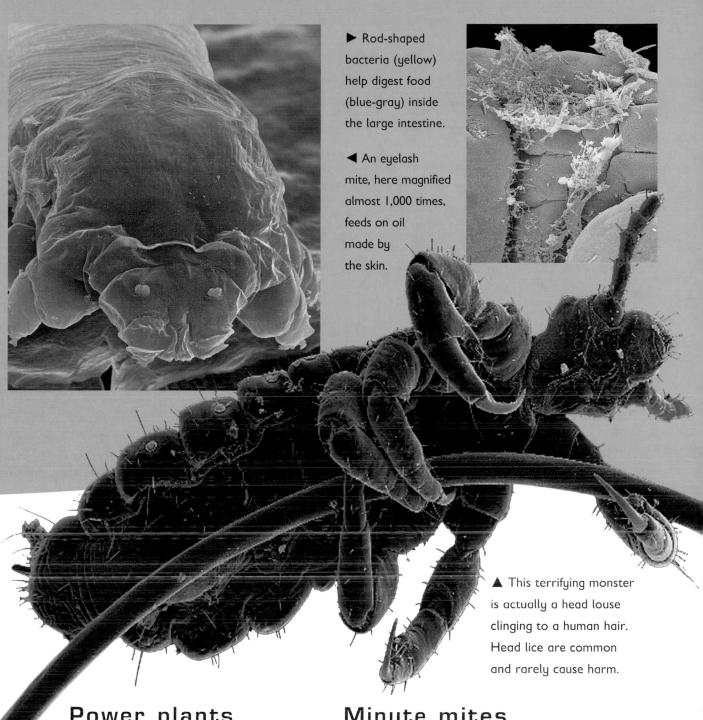

▶ Rod-shaped bacteria (yellow) help digest food (blue-gray) inside the large intestine.

◀ An eyelash mite, here magnified almost 1,000 times, feeds on oil made by the skin.

▲ This terrifying monster is actually a head louse clinging to a human hair. Head lice are common and rarely cause harm.

Power plants

In every cell of your body mitochondria can be found, working hard like tiny power plants to release energy for the cell. But millions of years ago these were separate creatures— an ancient type of bacteria.

Minute mites

Tiny mites live in the pores of the skin and in the roots of hairs, especially on the face and in the eyelashes. The mites feed on dead skin cells and oil made by glands. Most people have these mites, but they rarely cause problems.

13

Blood

Blood is the liquid of life. It flows around the body in tubes called blood vessels, taking food and oxygen to every cell and collecting waste. Blood also helps maintain the body's temperature. It contains millions of tiny cells that float in a liquid called plasma.

▲ This bag of blood could save someone's life! But it can only be given to a person who has the same blood type.

Red is the color

Almost all of the cells in your blood are red blood cells, which give blood its color. These cells carry oxygen around the body. A red blood cell is shaped like a doughnut without a hole. This shape helps them collect oxygen in the lungs and transport it to cells in the tissues.

▼ A white blood cell surrounds and destroys harmful bacteria (red).

Search and destroy

White blood cells keep you safe from infections. They prowl around the body, hunting for germs such as bacteria. Some white blood cells make chemicals that can kill the germs. Others surround the germs and swallow them.

▲ Blood, made up of red and white blood cells, rushes through a blood vessel. The blood cells are carried in plasma.

Info lab

- Only one in every 700 blood cells is a white blood cell.

- In one drop of blood there are around 250 million red blood cells.

Blood givers

Without enough blood, the tissues in the body are starved of oxygen and die. If you are hurt in an accident and lose blood, you could be saved by a blood transfusion. This is blood given by other people that is then stored for emergencies.

▶ To make a clot, tiny blood cells, called platelets (pale green), trigger the formation of a net of threads that trap both red and white blood cells.

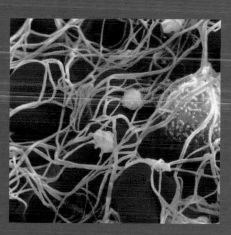

▶ If you cut your skin, blood cells escape from damaged blood vessels.

▶ A blood clot quickly forms, making a plug that stops the bleeding.

▶ As the skin repairs itself, the clot shrinks to form a scab on the surface.

Heal yourself

If you fall over and bump your knee, the wound will stop bleeding after a little while. This is because blood can form a clot, or sticky lump, that plugs the holes in the broken blood vessels.

Sending blood around the body

Every minute of every day blood travels completely around your body through a network of blood vessels. Blood is pumped through the blood vessels by the heart, which is found in the middle of your chest.

▲ A doctor is checking this boy's pulse. Every time the heart beats it makes a blood vessel pulse on the inside of the wrist.

Two sides

The heart is a strong muscular bag, around as big as your clenched fist. It is divided into two halves, left and right. Each half is made up of two chambers. The upper chamber is called the atrium, and the lower chamber is the ventricle.

Pumping machine

Every time the heart beats, it squeezes blood out through blood vessels called arteries. This pushing force, called blood pressure, is very strong, so the arteries have thick walls. Blood returns to the heart through the veins. The heart is no longer under much pressure, so veins do not need to be as strong as arteries.

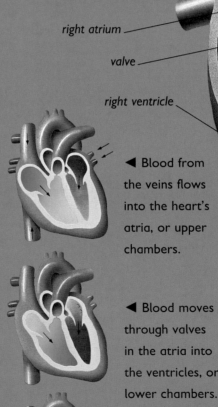

right atrium

valve

right ventricle

◀ Blood from the veins flows into the heart's atria, or upper chambers.

◀ Blood moves through valves in the atria into the ventricles, or lower chambers.

◀ The ventricles pump blood back out to the lungs and the rest of the body.

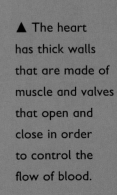

▲ The heart has thick walls that are made of muscle and valves that open and close in order to control the flow of blood.

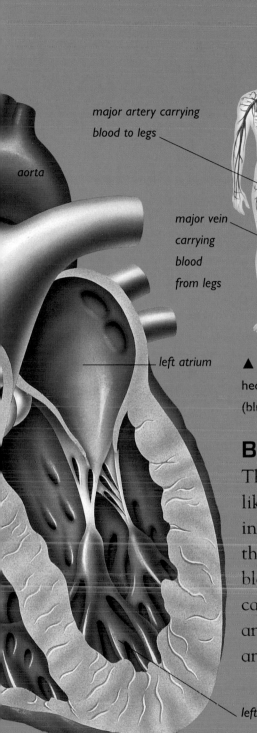

aorta

heart

major artery carrying blood to legs

major vein carrying blood from legs

left atrium

left ventricle

capillaries

▲ Arteries (red) carry blood from the heart to the rest of the body. Veins (blue) carry blood back to the heart.

Branching out

The main arteries divide like the branches of a tree into smaller arteries and then into capillaries. As blood passes through the capillaries, it releases food and oxygen to the cells and collects waste.

▲ When you exercise, more blood is pumped by the heart to the skin. This helps prevent the body from overheating—and it also makes your cheeks pink.

◄ Blood flows between the arteries (red) and the veins (blue) through a network of tiny tubes called capillaries.

Get active

Give your heart a workout! When you exercise, your muscles use up more oxygen and food, and your heart has to work much harder in order to keep them supplied with blood. It may pump up to five times more blood around the body.

Fighting infections

There is a war going on in your body! It is constantly under attack from germs that can cause infections and make you sick. But your body has many ways to protect itself, including barriers, killer cells, and chemicals that are poisonous to germs.

▲ These rod-shaped bacteria are being swallowed up by a white blood cell (orange).

On the defense

To get inside the body, germs, such as bacteria and viruses, have to get past a number of defenses. The skin forms the first line of defense. There the cells are packed closely together to stop microorganisms from getting through. In the nose thick mucus traps germs. Body fluids, including tears, saliva, and sweat, contain chemicals that kill bacteria.

The hunters

White blood cells are natural killers! Some cells move between the bloodstream and the tissues looking for germs. When they find one, they may release chemicals that kill the germ, or they might wrap themselves around their prey and digest it.

▼ These bacteria, called streptococci, can cause serious infections. They build an outer shell in order to protect themselves against the body's white blood cells.

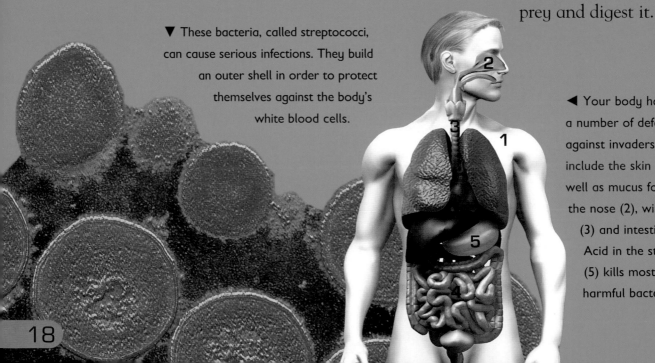

◀ Your body has a number of defenses against invaders. These include the skin (1), as well as mucus found in the nose (2), windpipe, (3) and intestines (4). Acid in the stomach (5) kills most harmful bacteria.

▲ This girl is being given a vaccination by a doctor. The vaccination will protect her from germs that can cause life-threatening infections.

Vaccines

For hundreds of years people feared infectious diseases that spread very quickly such as smallpox or the plague. Since the development of vaccines in the late 1700s and antibiotic medicines in the 1920s, millions of lives have been saved.

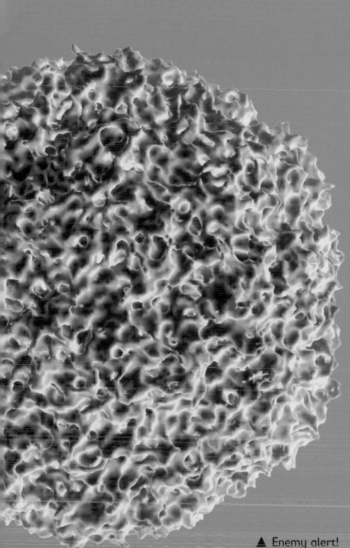
▲ Enemy alert! Viruses like this one, here magnified thousands of times, can invade your body through the nose and cause a cold.

▶ The first microscope was invented more than 300 years ago. It allowed scientists to see bacteria.

Antibodies

When germs enter the body and cause an infection, special white blood cells, called lymphocytes, learn to recognize the intruders. The next time the same type of germ invades the lymphocytes spot them and release chemicals called antibodies to stop the germs in their tracks.

Info lab

- Breast milk contains antibodies that protect a baby from infections.

- Your temperature increases during an infection to try to stop the germs from reproducing.

19

Digesting food

Your body needs food for energy, growth, and repair. But first the food needs to be digested, or broken down. This is the job of your digestive system. The mouth, stomach, and intestines work together to break down food into tiny particles called nutrients.

◄ Digestion begins in the mouth. Teeth cut up and crush food. The lips and tongue help hold food or move it around.

◄ After you swallow food strong muscles in the wall of the esophagus squeeze it down toward the stomach.

Food crushers

Your teeth are powerful crushers that can chew and cut through tough pieces of food. Saliva, or spit, contains chemicals that also help digest the food.

Stretchy stomach

The stomach is a stretchy but strong muscular bag. It churns and squeezes the food that you have swallowed. Fluids, called digestive juices, help break up the food, which can stay in the stomach for several hours before passing into the intestines.

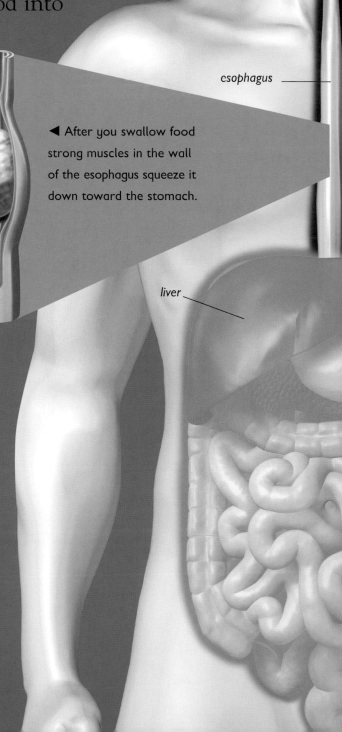

esophagus

liver

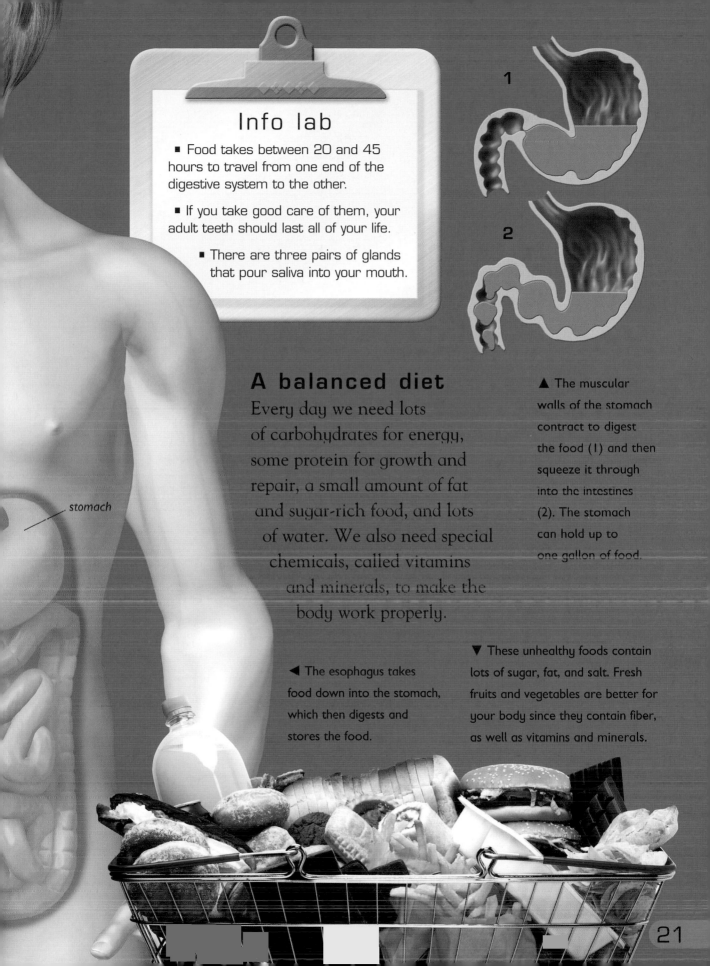

Info lab

■ Food takes between 20 and 45 hours to travel from one end of the digestive system to the other.

■ If you take good care of them, your adult teeth should last all of your life.

■ There are three pairs of glands that pour saliva into your mouth.

stomach

A balanced diet

Every day we need lots of carbohydrates for energy, some protein for growth and repair, a small amount of fat and sugar-rich food, and lots of water. We also need special chemicals, called vitamins and minerals, to make the body work properly.

▲ The muscular walls of the stomach contract to digest the food (1) and then squeeze it through into the intestines (2). The stomach can hold up to one gallon of food.

◄ The esophagus takes food down into the stomach, which then digests and stores the food.

▼ These unhealthy foods contain lots of sugar, fat, and salt. Fresh fruits and vegetables are better for your body since they contain fiber, as well as vitamins and minerals.

The intestines

When food leaves the stomach, it enters the small intestine, where it is broken down into smaller and smaller particles. The food, now in the form of tiny nutrients, moves through the small intestine and into the bloodstream. The waste matter that is left is pushed out through the anus.

Down the tube

The small intestine is a 20-ft. (6-m)-long tube where food is absorbed, or taken into the body. It is lined with millions of tiny hairlike projections called villi. These form a large surface through which nutrients can pass into the blood vessels beneath.

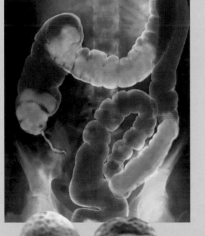

◀ The large intestine is around 5 ft. (1.5m) long. Its main job is to get rid of waste.

▼ Tiny villi cover the inside of the small intestine. Nutrients pass through them and into the blood.

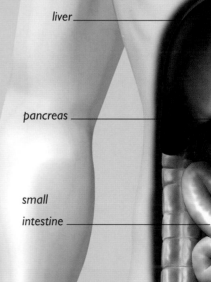

liver

pancreas

small intestine

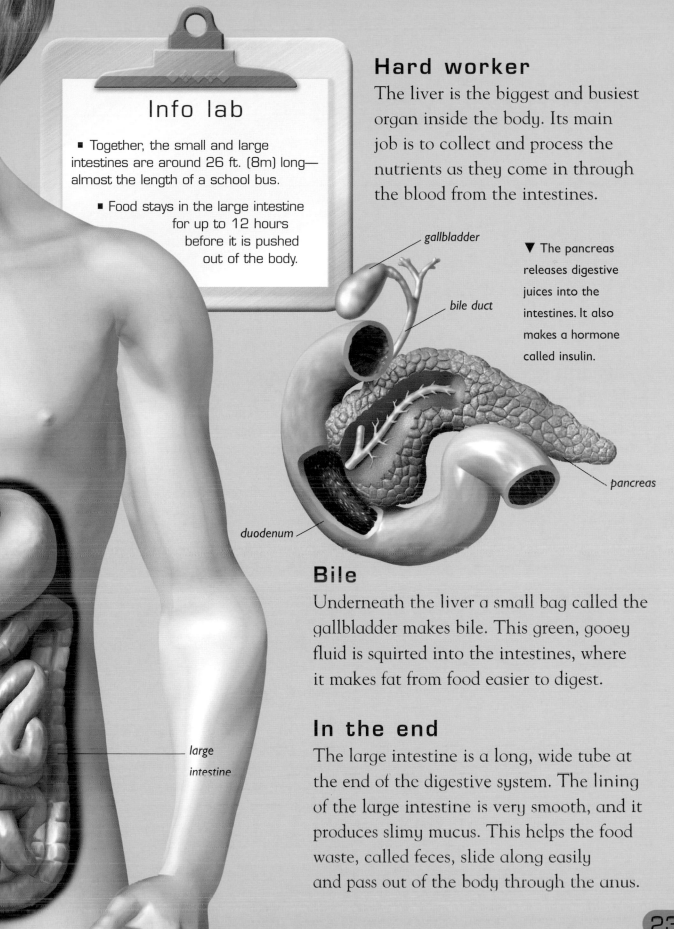

Hard worker

The liver is the biggest and busiest organ inside the body. Its main job is to collect and process the nutrients as they come in through the blood from the intestines.

Info lab

- Together, the small and large intestines are around 26 ft. (8m) long— almost the length of a school bus.

- Food stays in the large intestine for up to 12 hours before it is pushed out of the body.

gallbladder

bile duct

▼ The pancreas releases digestive juices into the intestines. It also makes a hormone called insulin.

pancreas

duodenum

large intestine

Bile

Underneath the liver a small bag called the gallbladder makes bile. This green, gooey fluid is squirted into the intestines, where it makes fat from food easier to digest.

In the end

The large intestine is a long, wide tube at the end of the digestive system. The lining of the large intestine is very smooth, and it produces slimy mucus. This helps the food waste, called feces, slide along easily and pass out of the body through the anus.

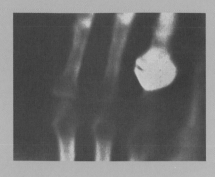

Imaging the body

Special medical tools allow doctors to peer deep inside the body. Many illnesses and diseases can be spotted without having to cut the body open.

▲ The first X-ray was made by Wilhelm Röntgen in 1895 and shows the bones of his wife's fingers. You can even see her wedding ring.

▼ This child has just had pictures taken of her internal organs by a machine called an MRI scanner.

Breakthrough

In 1895 a German doctor named Wilhelm Röntgen discovered X-rays. X-rays are a type of energy, called radiation, that passes through soft tissues but not bone. They are still used today to detect broken bones.

Wave pictures

Magnetic resonance imaging, or MRI, uses magnetism and radio waves to scan the body. A computer looks at how the waves are bent and then creates an accurate picture of the inside of the body.

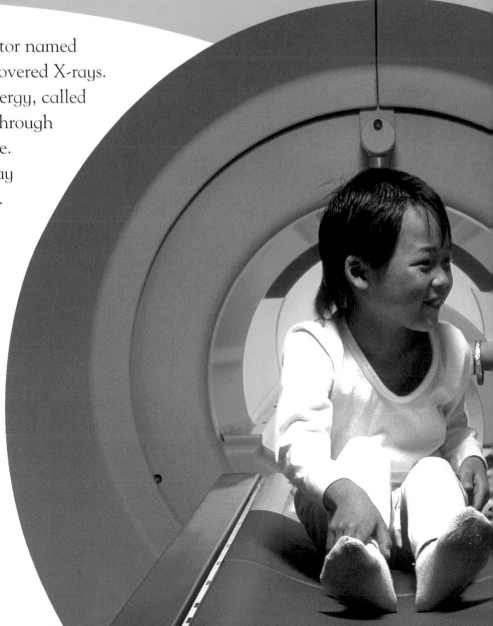

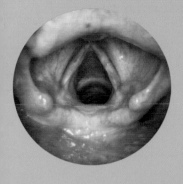

▲ An endoscope—a tiny camera attached to a tube—took this picture showing the larynx, or voice box.

Inside job

Doctors can check organs and tissues using an endoscope. This instrument has a tiny camera attached to a bendable tube. It can easily be inserted into the body through the mouth or a specially-made cut in the skin.

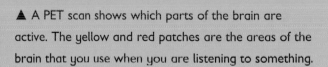

▶ X-rays and MRI scans have been used to create this image of different parts of the body.

▲ A PET scan shows which parts of the brain are active. The yellow and red patches are the areas of the brain that you use when you are listening to something.

Mysteries of the brain

The brain has been one of the most difficult areas of the body to take pictures of because it is hidden away inside the hard case of the skull. But a type of scan called a PET (positron-emission tomography) scan can detect which parts of the brain are being used at any moment in time.

Breath of life

Your respiratory, or breathing, system, which includes the nose, throat, and lungs, takes oxygen from the air and delivers it to your blood. The oxygen is then transported to your body's cells. Without oxygen, your cells would die—they need this gas to release energy from food.

Breathe in

Put your hands on your chest as you inhale, or breathe in, and feel your lungs fill up with air. Two sets of muscles draw air into your lungs— the muscles of the rib cage and a large, flat muscle under the lungs called the diaphragm.

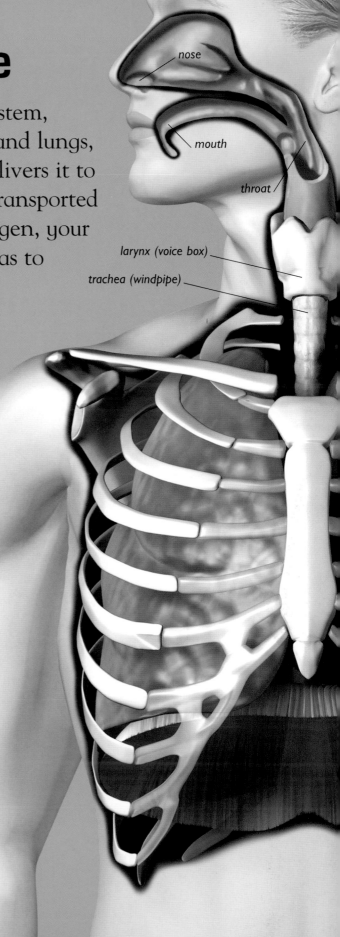

nose

mouth

throat

larynx (voice box)

trachea (windpipe)

▲ When you breathe in, the space inside your chest becomes larger and pulls air into the lungs.

▲ When you breathe out, the space inside your chest becomes smaller, and air is pushed out of your lungs.

No entry

The larynx, or voice box, is located at the entrance to the trachea—the main tube into the lungs. A flap of tissue inside the larynx prevents food from getting into the lungs. This flap is called the epiglottis.

Making sounds

The larynx also contains two folds of mucous membranes called the vocal cords. When you breathe, air is squeezed past the folds, making the vocal cords vibrate. This produces sounds that can be shaped into words by moving your tongue and lips.

▼ When you sing or speak, the vocal cords inside your larynx vibrate to make sounds. The vocal cords are two folds in the shape of a "V."

lungs

rib cage

diaphragm

The lungs

Your lungs are a pair of large, spongy organs inside the chest. They are protected by the bones and muscles that form the rib cage. Inside the lungs are millions of tiny air bags that pass oxygen into the blood. The lungs also breathe out a waste gas called carbon dioxide.

Forest of tubes

Your lungs are connected to the outside world by your trachea. The lower end of this long tube divides into two parts, each one entering a lung. In the lungs the tubes continue to divide like the branches of a tree into smaller and smaller tubes. The narrowest ones end in tiny air bags called alveoli.

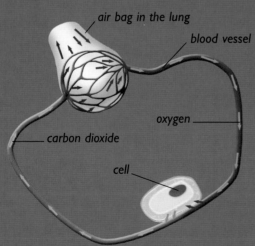

air bag in the lung

blood vessel

oxygen

carbon dioxide

cell

▲ Oxygen in the lungs is carried by the blood to the body's cells. Carbon dioxide waste is removed from the cells and breathed out.

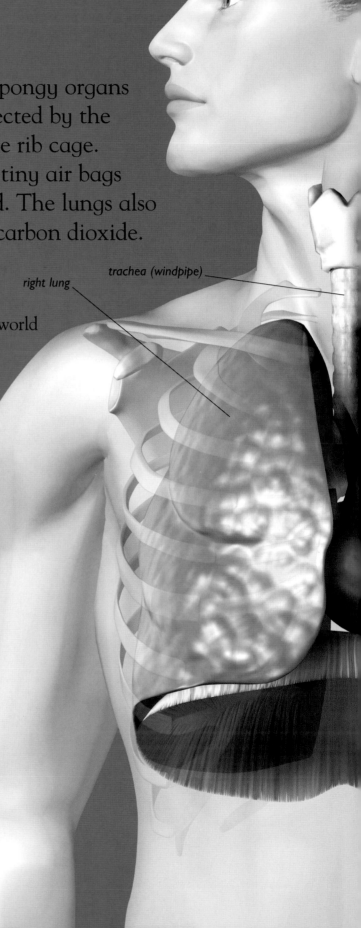

trachea (windpipe)

right lung

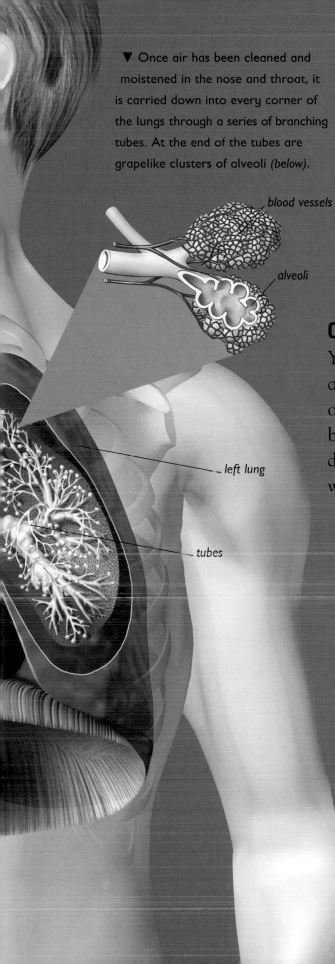

▼ Once air has been cleaned and moistened in the nose and throat, it is carried down into every corner of the lungs through a series of branching tubes. At the end of the tubes are grapelike clusters of alveoli (below).

blood vessels

alveoli

left lung

tubes

Gas exchange

Your lungs contain more than 300 million alveoli. Each one is covered in a network of blood vessels that carry oxygen into the bloodstream. The alveoli also take carbon dioxide from the blood into the lungs, where it can be exhaled, or breathed out.

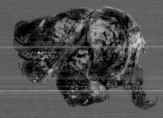

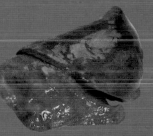

▲ This is a lung from a person who smokes. It is full of harmful chemicals, which have turned the lung black.

▲ Healthy lungs are clean and pink.

Bad habit

Healthy lungs are smooth, pink, and shiny. But the lungs of a smoker are dark and dirty. Smoking damages the lungs and prevents them from working properly. This makes breathing more difficult.

Living and working in outer space

In space there is no air or food! Astronauts need to take supplies of food, water, and oxygen with them. But there is not much room inside a spaceship, and every extra item increases the amount of fuel needed for takeoff. So scientists have come up with ingenious ways to make sure that astronauts get enough food and oxygen.

▲ In space gravity is weaker than on Earth. This makes everything—from astronauts to candy—weightless.

▼ Outside the spaceship an astronaut wears a portable life-support system. This provides a steady supply of oxygen.

▲ Food supplies are dried and carefully packaged.
Fresh food weighs much more and does not last as long.

Space meals

Before the mission meals are carefully planned and prepared to make sure that each astronaut gets all of the nutrients and energy they need. Most of the food is processed and packaged. It is made to look like freshly prepared food so it is more appetizing.

Space toilets

Gravity is very weak in space, so unless you are careful, your food, drinks, and even your body's waste products could float around the cabin! Astronauts use a special toilet that uses air, rather than water, to force the waste into a collection bag.

▶ This toilet was specially designed for the U.S. space station *Freedom*. The astronauts strap themselves to the seat to make a tight seal.

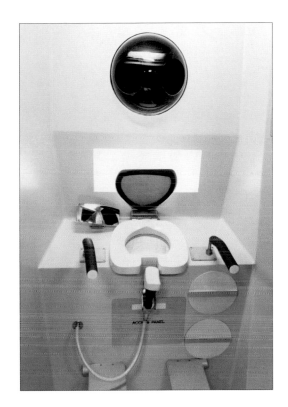

Air supplies

On short trips into space air is supplied from tanks of oxygen on the spacecraft. But on longer journeys most of the oxygen is made by a machine that uses electricity to split water into hydrogen gas and oxygen gas. Scientists are also researching ways of using plants to produce oxygen.

Water cycle

On the International Space Station almost every drop of water is recycled. Most of it is collected from the air that the astronauts breathe out. Water is even recycled from the urine of the station's laboratory animals!

Cleaning up

While your body is busy making energy, building new cells, and repairing old ones, it needs to get rid of waste products. If these are allowed to build up, they can poison the body. However, you have some clever cleaning systems to get rid of this waste.

Cleaning blood

Waste chemicals are carried away from the cells by the blood. The blood is cleaned by your two kidneys. Each one contains more than 500,000 tiny filters that sift out harmful substances and remove excess water. The waste fluid, called urine, drains out of the kidneys through the ureter into the bladder.

▶ Inside each kidney (shown here cut in half lengthwise) the medulla and cortex contain tiny filters. These clean the blood and remove water that is not needed by the body.

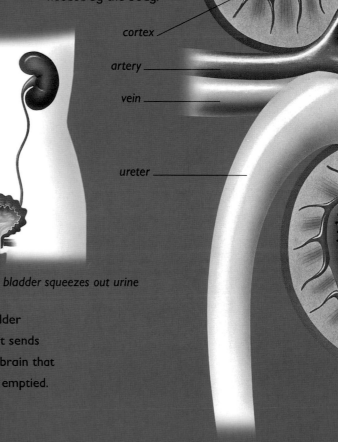

medulla

cortex

artery

vein

ureter

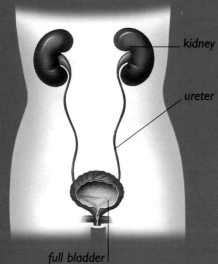

kidney

ureter

full bladder

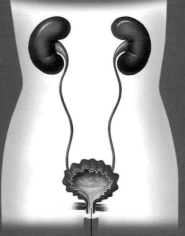

bladder squeezes out urine

▲ Urine drains from the kidneys down long tubes, called ureters, into the bladder.

▲ As the bladder becomes full, it sends signals to the brain that it needs to be emptied.

The liver

Some waste chemicals or cells are broken down by the liver, which is the recycling factory of the body. The leftovers are then used again to make new cells. The liver also breaks down chemicals that may be dangerous such as alcohol or drugs.

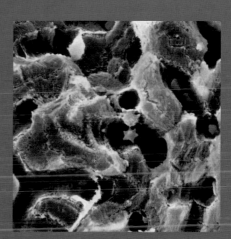

▶ In the liver blood flows through channels between rows of liver cells. As well as breaking down poisonous chemicals, the liver stores vitamins.

Hot and sweaty

When we are hot, more blood is sent to the surface of the body so that heat can be lost through the skin. We also sweat, which helps cool the skin and remove extra water, salt, and an important waste chemical called urea from the body.

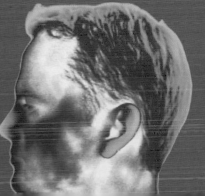

▶ The body gets rid of excess heat through the skin. In this picture, called a thermogram, the hottest areas, such as the cheeks, show up as red, while cooler skin appears blue.

The skin

Imagine being a tiny creature on a person's skin. You would have to struggle through a jungle of hairs, avoiding dozens of potholes or pores oozing sweat! Skin is the body's largest and heaviest organ. It is tough and waterproof, and it helps stop germs and dirt from entering the body.

▲ We each have a unique pattern of fingerprints on the tips of our fingers. Try comparing yours with your friends' fingerprints.

Fingerprints

Everybody's fingerprints are unique. Even if you damage your fingers, the fingerprints will grow back in the same pattern. The ridges that form fingerprints have hundreds of sweat glands that help keep your skin cool.

► This is a magnified picture of hairs emerging from skin on the face. Hair can grow up to 6 in. (15cm) per year.

◄ There are many different shades of skin color. But beneath the epidermis, or top layer, we all look very similar.

Toolbox

Fingernails provide a set of tough tools that are very useful for jobs that involve scraping and gripping. Nails are made from dead cells and a very tough substance called keratin.

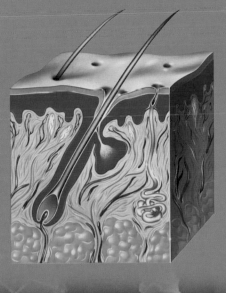

◀ The skin has a range of different sensors. Light touch and pressure are detected by sensors close to the surface.

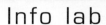
Body hair

The hair on the top of your head is thick, but much finer hairs cover most of your body. These hairs let you sense very light touch. Your eyebrows help keep sweat from dripping into your eyes, and eyelashes protect them from dust.

So sensitive

The skin is covered with millions of tiny nerves. The endings of these nerves work as sensors that can detect pressure, pain, and other sensations. This information is sent to the brain.

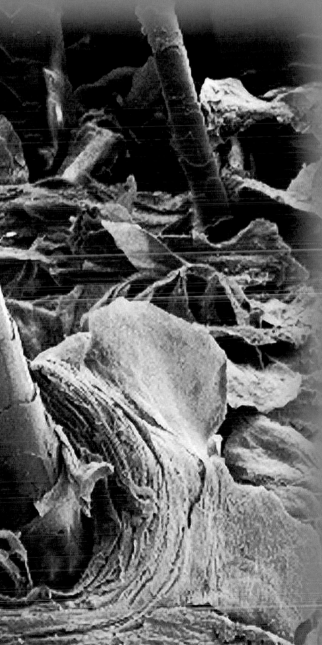

▶ Fingerprints can help catch criminals! The police take fingerprints from suspects and see if these match prints found at the scene of the crime.

Glossary

artery A blood vessel that carries blood from the heart to the rest of the body.

bladder A hollow, muscular organ that collects urine from the kidneys and stores it before passing it from the body.

blood vessels
Tubes that carry blood around the body—arteries, veins, or capillaries, for example.

capillaries The smallest blood vessels in the body. In the capillaries oxygen moves from the blood into the cells.

carbon dioxide A colorless gas made by the cells of the body and breathed out by the lungs.

cell The smallest unit found in any living organism. Every tissue and organ in the human body is made up of a collection of cells.

chromosomes
Microscopic threads found in cells. They are made of a chemical called DNA and contain the genes. Each cell has 46 chromosomes.

diaphragm A dome-shaped sheet of muscle below the lungs that plays an important part in breathing.

DNA The chemical found in each cell that carries information about how to build and run the body. DNA is stored in the chromosomes.

immune system The collection of cells in the body that work together to fight diseases.

intestines A long tube running from the stomach to the end of the digestive system where food is turned into a liquid and nutrients pass into the bloodstream.

kidney One of two large, bean-shaped organs that clean the blood and make urine in order to get rid of waste products and excess fluid.

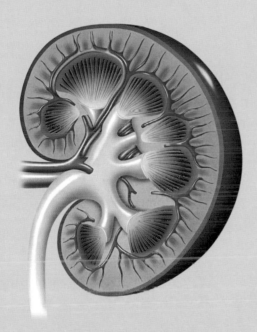

microorganisms Tiny living things that can only be seen under a microscope such as bacteria, viruses, and fungi.

nucleus The control center of a cell.

organ A major part of the body such as the heart, lungs, or kidneys. An organ is made up of different tissues and carries out a specific task.

oxygen A colorless gas taken into the bloodstream from air in the lungs. It is used by cells to release energy from food and is essential for life.

saliva Fluid made in the mouth. It moistens food and starts the digestion process.

tissue A part of the body formed by cells of a similar type. Each type of tissue, such as muscle tissue or nerve tissue, carries out a specific job.

trachea A long tube, also known as the windpipe, that carries air from the back of the throat down into the lungs.

vein A blood vessel that carries blood from the body back to the heart.

vitamin Chemicals contained in foods. The body needs tiny amounts of vitamins in order to work properly.

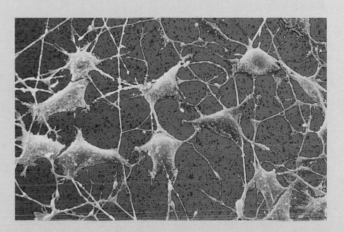

Index

Web sites

Kidshealth has lots of information about your body's organs: www.kidshealth.org/kid/body/

Find out how your body systems run with the help of cartoons, quizzes, and fun facts: www.brainpop.com/health/

Learn where your organs are found and what they do at the BBC's interactive site: www.bbc.co.uk/science/humanbody/body/index.shtml

Discover digestion, breathing, and other body systems at: http://yucky.kids.discovery.com/flash/body/pg000029.html

For an introduction to cells, genes, and DNA, try these two sites: http://ology.amnh.org/genetics/index.html and www.genecrc.org/site/ko/index_ko.htm

Find out everything you ever wanted to know about blood: http://www.idahoptv.org/dialogue4kids/season4/blood/facts.html

Take a grand tour of the human body here: www.vilenski.org/science/humanbody/index.html

This web site looks at all of the different systems and organs in the body: http://library.thinkquest.org/5777/tour.htm?tqskip1=1

Acknowledgments

The publisher would like to thank the following for permission to reproduce their material. Every care has been taken to trace copyright holders. However, if there have been unintentional omissions or failure to trace copyright holders, we apologize and will, if informed, endeavor to make corrections in any future edition.

Key: b = bottom, c = center, l = left, r = right, t = top

Cover Patrik Giardino/Corbis; page 4 Dr. Arthur Tucker/SPL; 6bl Sygma/Corbis; 7 Chuck Savage/Corbis; 8tl David Becker/Science Photo Library (SPL); 8br ISM/SPL; 9cr VVG/SPL; 10tc VVG/SPL; 10tr VVG/SPL; 10cc Eye of Science/SPL; 10cr VVG/SPL; 11 Patrik Giardino/Corbis; 12tl Biophoto Associates/SPL; 12cr Comstock; 12bl Mona Lisa Productions/SPL; 13tl Andrew Syred/SPL; 13tr VVG/SPL; 13b VVG/SPL; 14tl Tek Image/SPL; 14bl SPL; 15tl VVG/SPL; 15r CNRI/SPL; 16tl CC Studio/SPL; 17 Chad Ehlers/ Alamy; 18tl Dr. Kari Lounatmaa/SPL; 18bl CNRI/SPL; 19tl Alfred Pasieka/SPL; 19tr Stone/ Getty Images; 20 Imagebank/Getty Images; 21 Imagebank/Getty Images; 22bl Eye of Science/SPL; 22l CNRI/SPL; 24tl SPL; 24–25 Imagebank/Getty Images; 25tl CNRI/SPL; 25r Mehau Kulyk/SPL; 25c Wellcome Institute/SPL; 27b Digital Vision/Getty Images; 29cl Matt Meadows, Peter Arnold Inc./SPL; 29cr Matt Meadows, Peter Arnold Inc./SPL; 30tl NASA/SPL; 30b Photodisc/Getty Images; 31tl Roger Ressmeyer/Corbis; 31r NASA/SPL; 33cr Professor Motta, La Spienze University, Rome/SPL; 33b Dr. Arthur Tucker/SPL; 34tr Maximilian Wienzerl/Alamy; 34–35 VVG/SPL; 34cl Laura Doss/Corbis; 35tl John Bavosi/SPL; 35br William Gottlieb/Corbis; 37 VVG/SPL; poster tl Digital Vision/Getty; b Patrik Giardino/Corbis